The Little Boo
PRESIDENTIAL
ELECTIONS

By Zack Bush and Laurie Friedman
Illustrated by Sarah Van Evera

DEDICATED TO YOU –
OUR WONDERFUL READER

THIS BOOK BELONGS TO:

 _____

Lately, you've probably heard a lot about the upcoming PRESIDENTIAL ELECTION.

Maybe you've seen news stories on TV.

Or stickers on cars.

And signs in yards.

These are signals that an ELECTION is near.
But what is a PRESIDENTIAL ELECTION?

By the time you get to the end of this book,
you will know all about the process of ELECTING
a president and why it is so important to VOTE.

Ready to learn?
Just turn
the page!

A PRESIDENTIAL ELECTION
is a very special time.
Why?

Because an ELECTION for the president of the United States only takes place once every four years.

A
PRESIDENTIAL
ELECTION
is the process of
VOTING
to choose someone
to be the leader of
our country. Every
person who has the
right to **VOTE** gets
to help choose who
will be president.

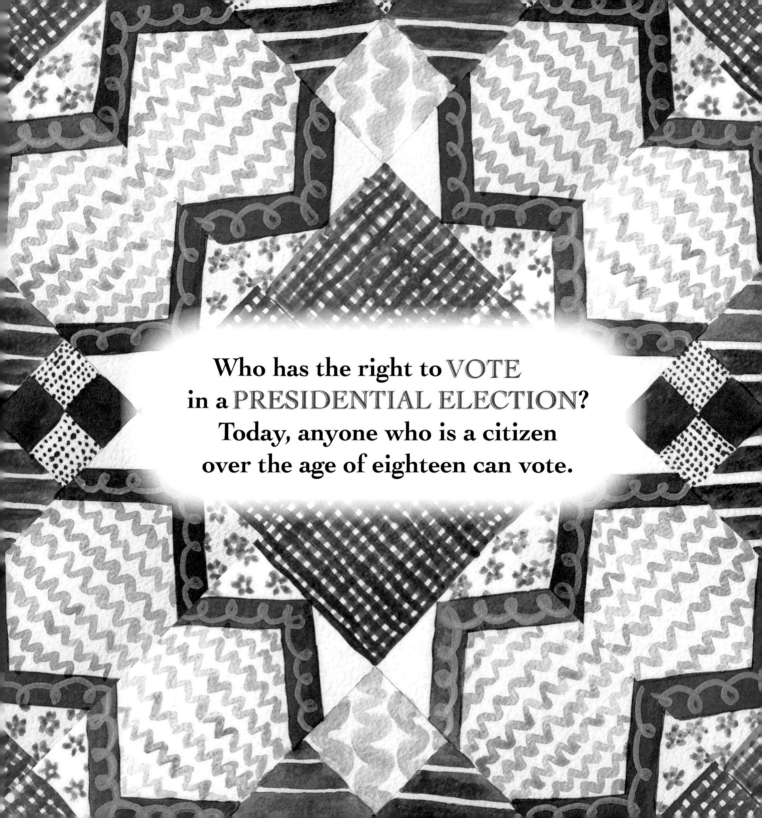

Who has the right to VOTE
in a PRESIDENTIAL ELECTION?
Today, anyone who is a citizen
over the age of eighteen can vote.

But even if you're not over eighteen, it's important to know who is running for president and what they stand for.

One day you will be able to VOTE too!

What does it mean
"to VOTE"?

Whoever has the most VOTES wins!

**Sometimes people disagree over
small decisions, like what's for dinner.**

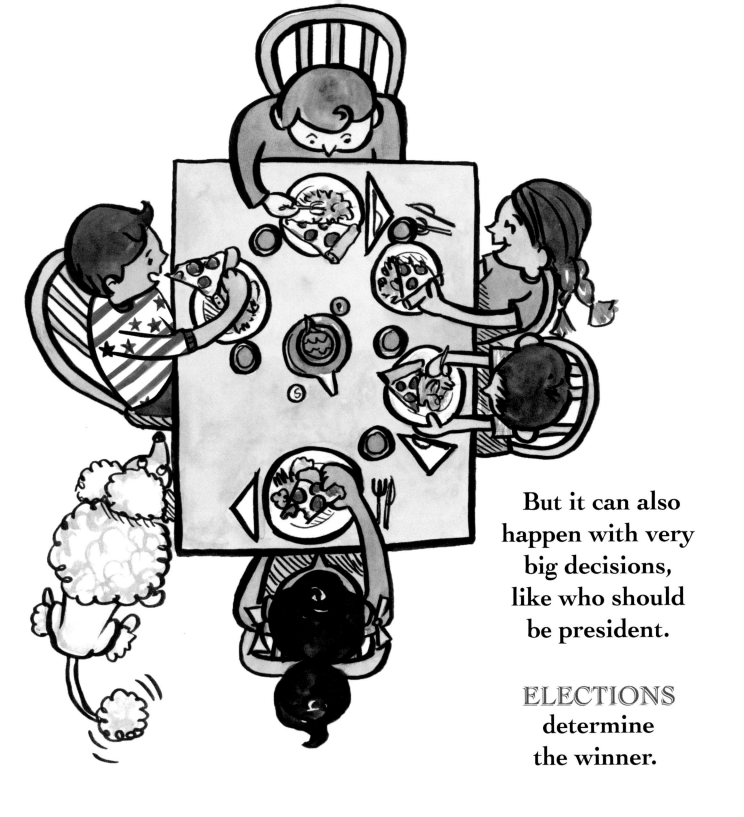

But it can also
happen with very
big decisions,
like who should
be president.

ELECTIONS
determine
the winner.

A PRESIDENTIAL ELECTION starts with candidates.

Candidates are the people running
against each other for president.

The candidates
give speeches
to let people
know what they
believe in and
why they think
they will be the best
person for the job.

Sometimes candidates disagree.
Sometimes they argue over important issues.

Having a difference of opinion is okay.

But it is important to be polite and respectful.
ALWAYS listen to what others have to say.
And if someone disagrees with you, it is important
to do your best to understand their point of view.

The PRESIDENTIAL ELECTION
begins with a primary election.

This is when the candidates who will run against each other are selected.

Once selected, the public then VOTES on which of the candidates they want to be their president.

Who is the public?

The public is people just like you and me.
When the public casts their VOTES,
this is called the popular VOTE.

You may think that the president of the United States is just VOTED on by all of the people in the country and the person with the most VOTES wins.

But it's not that simple.

The president is actually elected by something called the Electoral College.

HERE'S HOW IT WORKS:

 The people in each state vote.

 "Electors" from that state cast their votes.

 The candidate with the most electoral votes wins the election and becomes president.

Being president is a big job.

The president should be a symbol of our country.
Our people. And our beliefs.

VOTING for the best
candidate for the job is a privilege.

Many people in the world don't have the right to VOTE.

But the United States is a democracy.
That means it is a government by the people.
In a democracy, the people VOTE for their leader.

This is one of the things that makes
the United States of America so special.

How do you decide who you want to VOTE for?

VOTING for the person who best represents the issues that matter to you is one of the most important things you can do.

It may seem like one VOTE won't make a difference,
but if everybody votes,
it adds up to a lot of voices being heard.

Remember . . .
every VOTE counts!

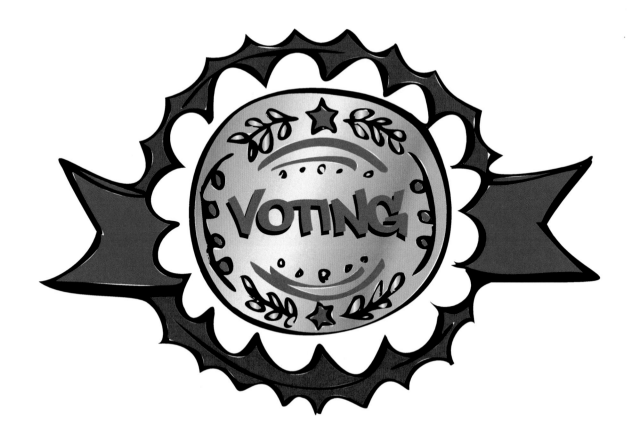

CONGRATULATIONS!

You've earned your VOTING BADGE.
Now you understand how presidential elections work
and why voting is a special privilege.

IMPORTANT TERMS TO KNOW:

PRESIDENTIAL ELECTION

The process of voting to choose someone to be the leader of our country.

CANDIDATE

The people running against each other for president.

PRIMARY ELECTION

When the candidates who will be running against each other are selected.

GENERAL ELECTION

When the people of the country cast their votes for president.

THE POPULAR VOTE

The candidate who gets the most votes nationwide is said to have won the popular vote.

ELECTORAL COLLEGE

Established by the founding fathers of our country as a way to make sure that presidential elections are fair.

ELECTORAL VOTE

The candidate who wins the most electoral votes wins the election.

DEMOCRACY

A government by the people.

Go to the website
www.BooksByZackAndLaurie.com
to print out your voting badge.
And keep reading all of the books in
#thelittlebookof
series to learn new things
and earn more badges.

Other books in the series:

The Little Book of Camping
The Little Book of Friendship
The Little Book of Kindness
The Little Book of Patience